Pat, Tap

by Holly Harper
illustrated by Debby Rahmalia

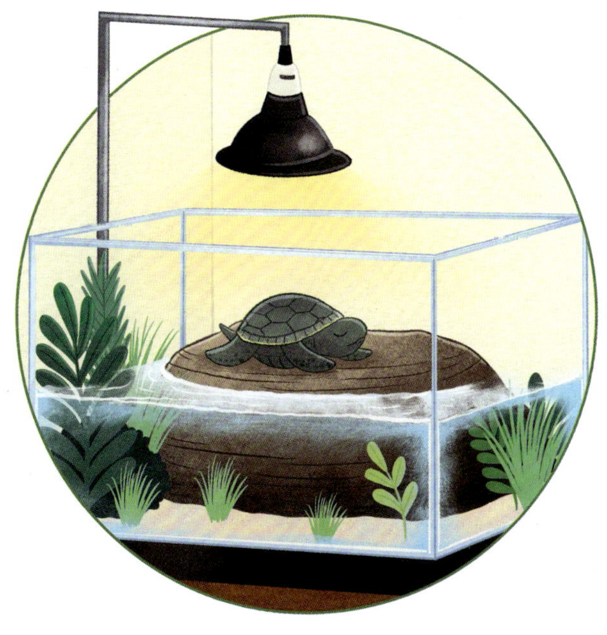

OXFORD
UNIVERSITY PRESS

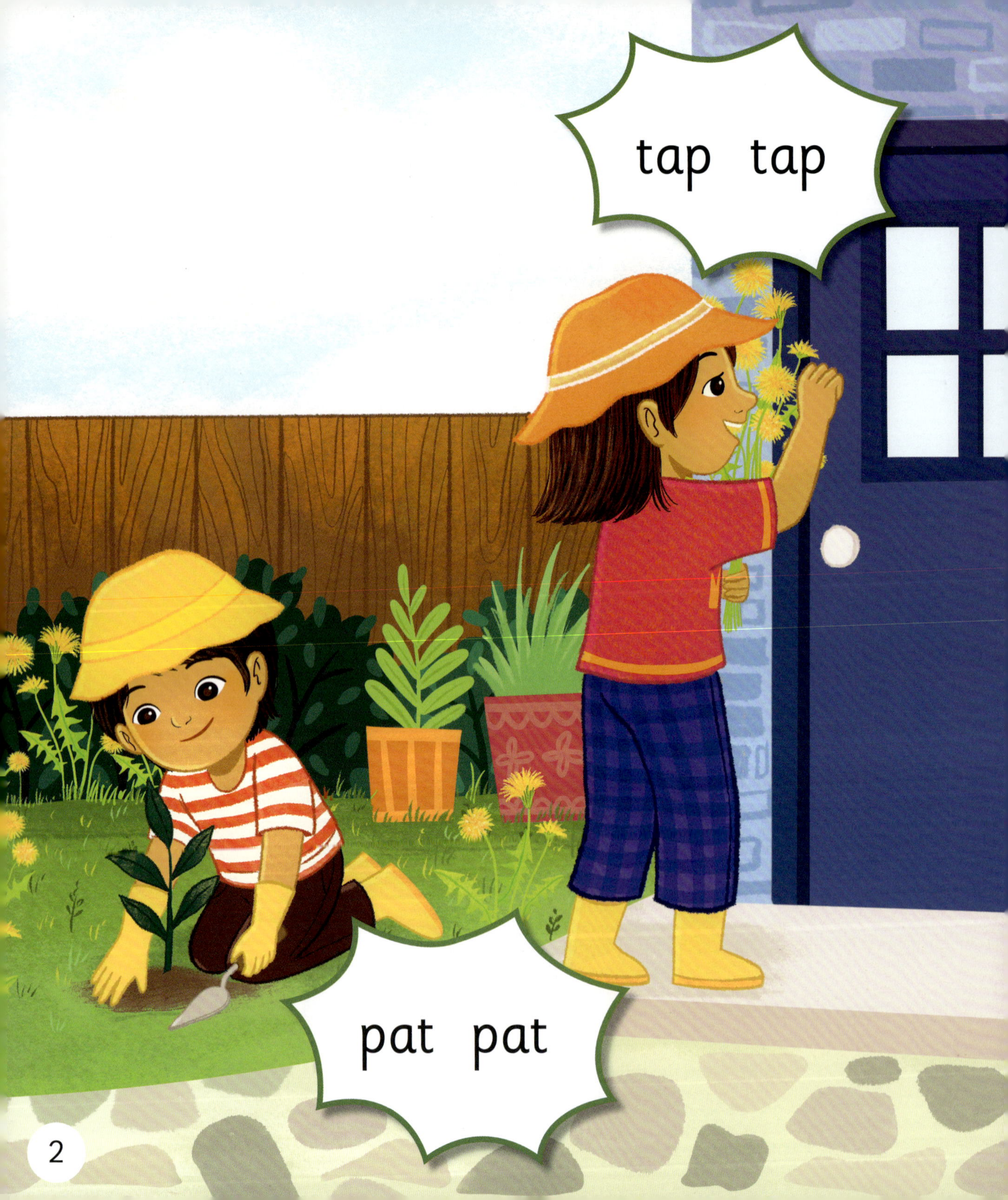
tap tap
pat pat

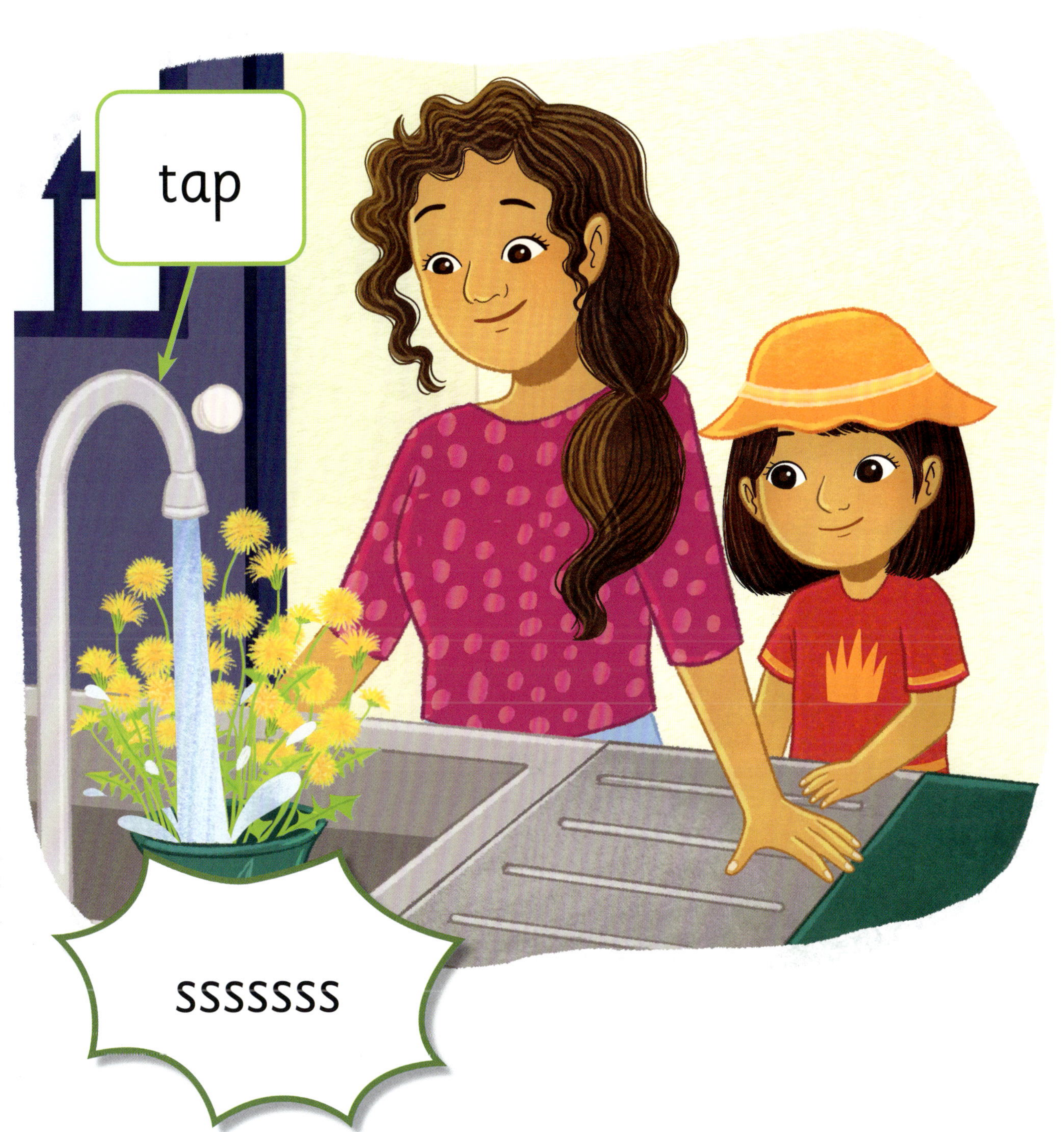
tap
sssssss

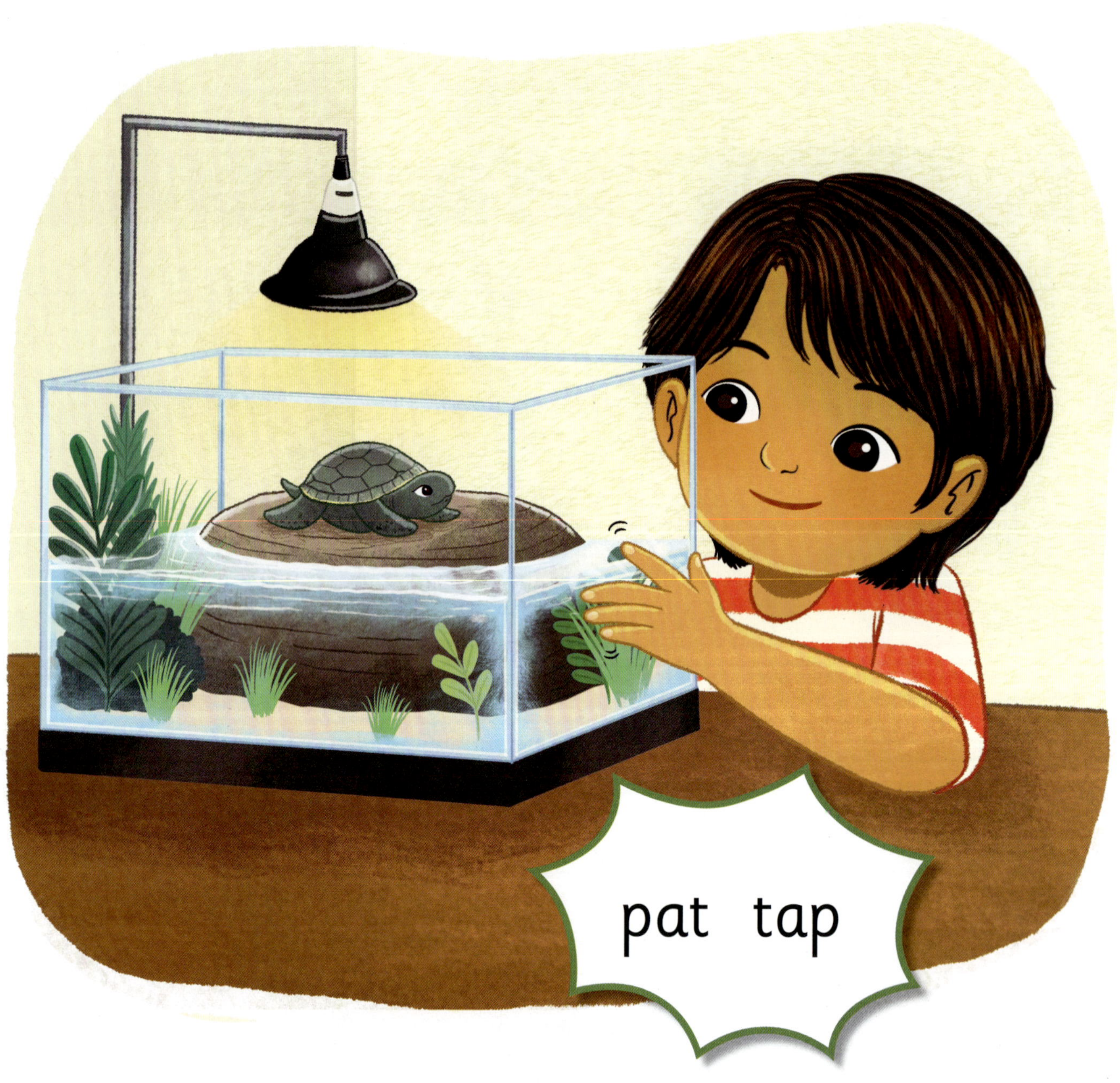
pat tap

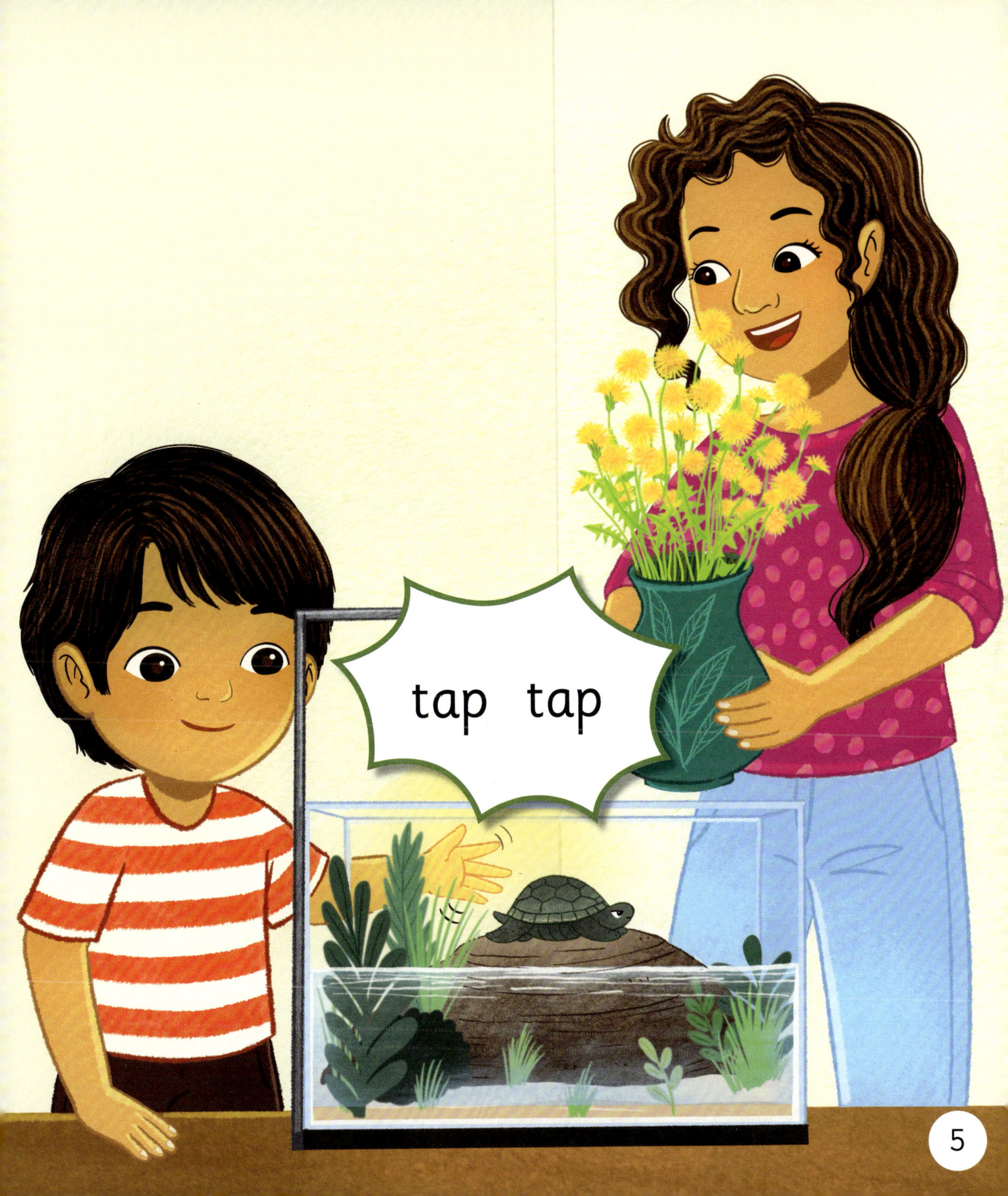
tap tap

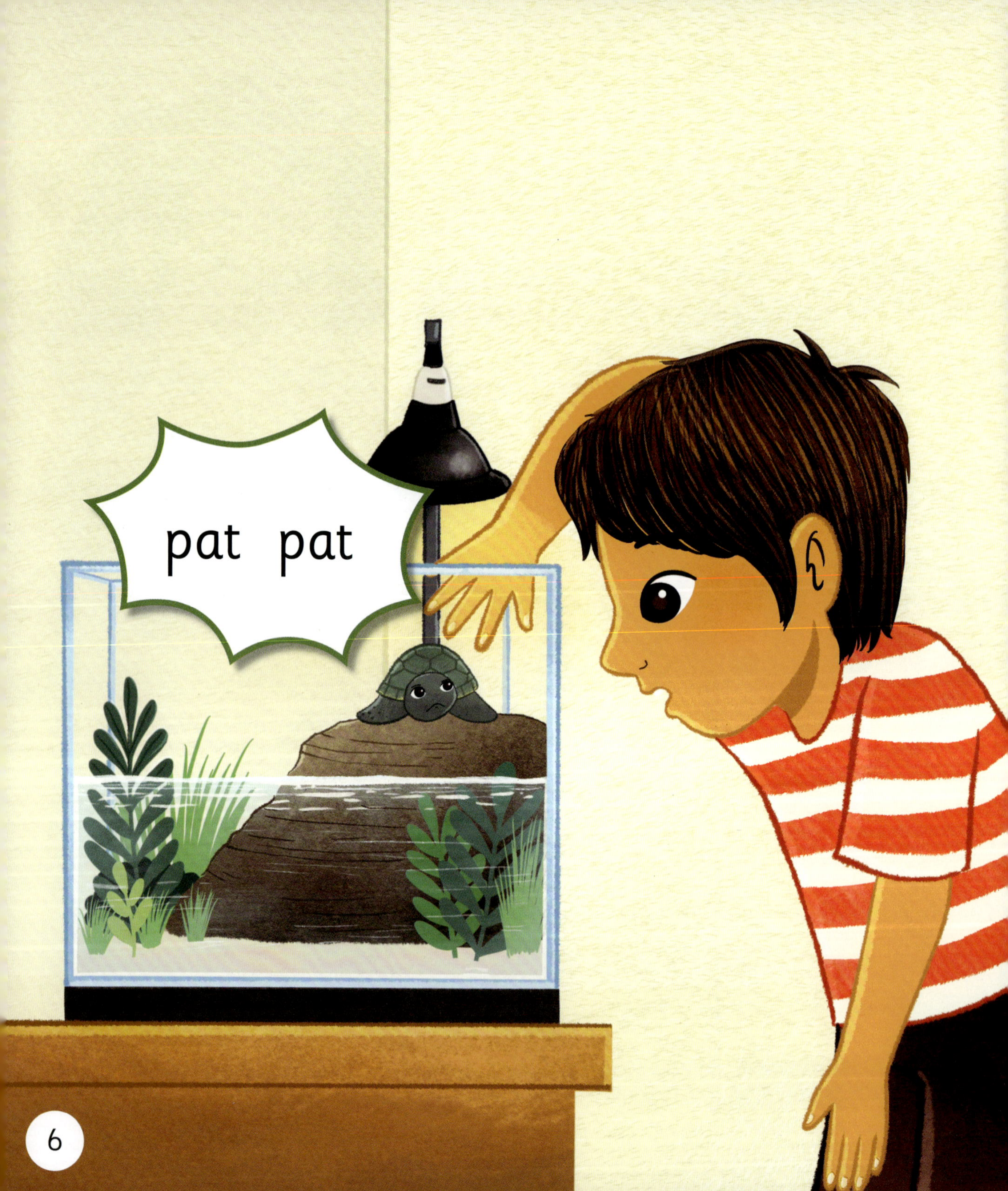
pat pat

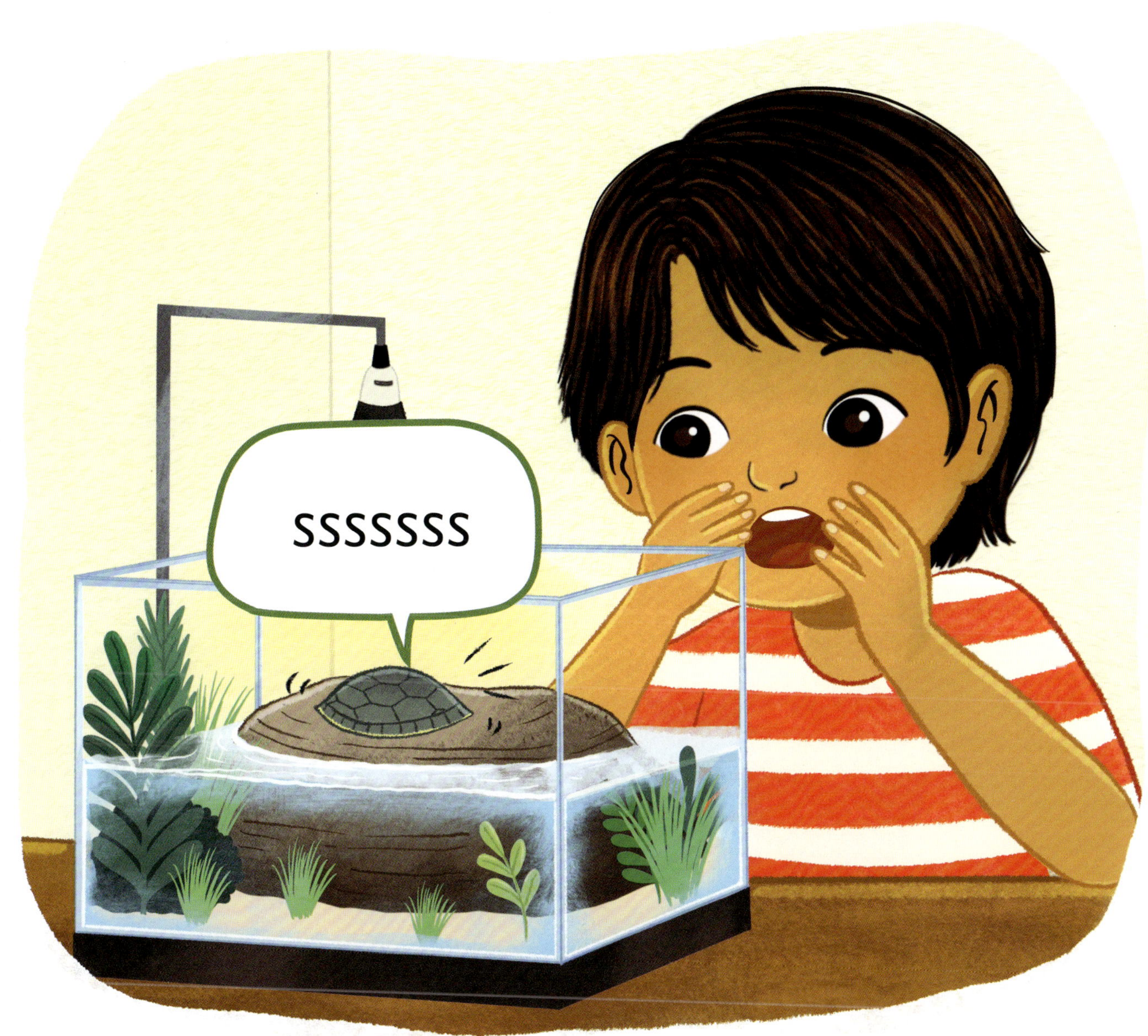
SSSSSSS

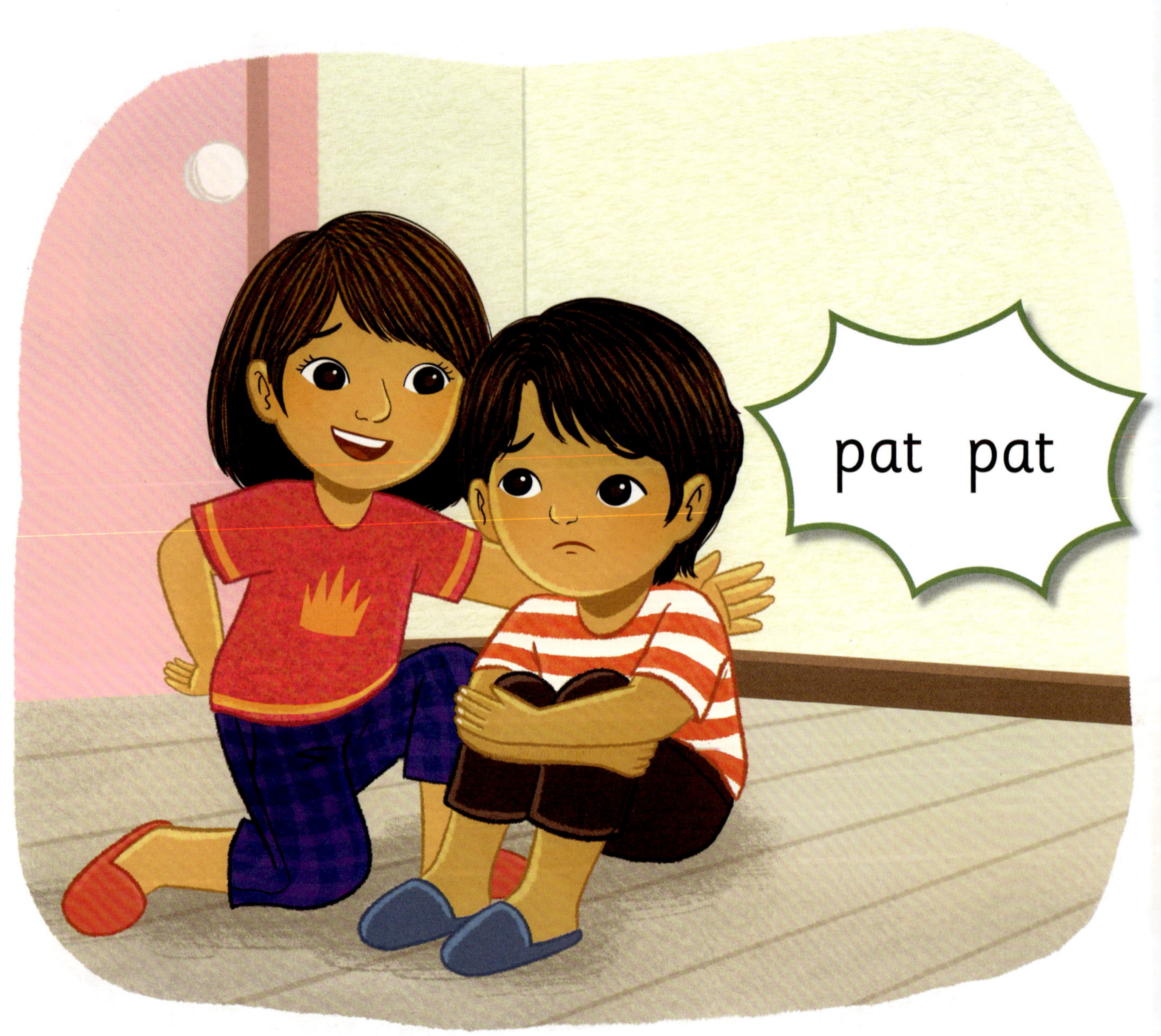
pat pat

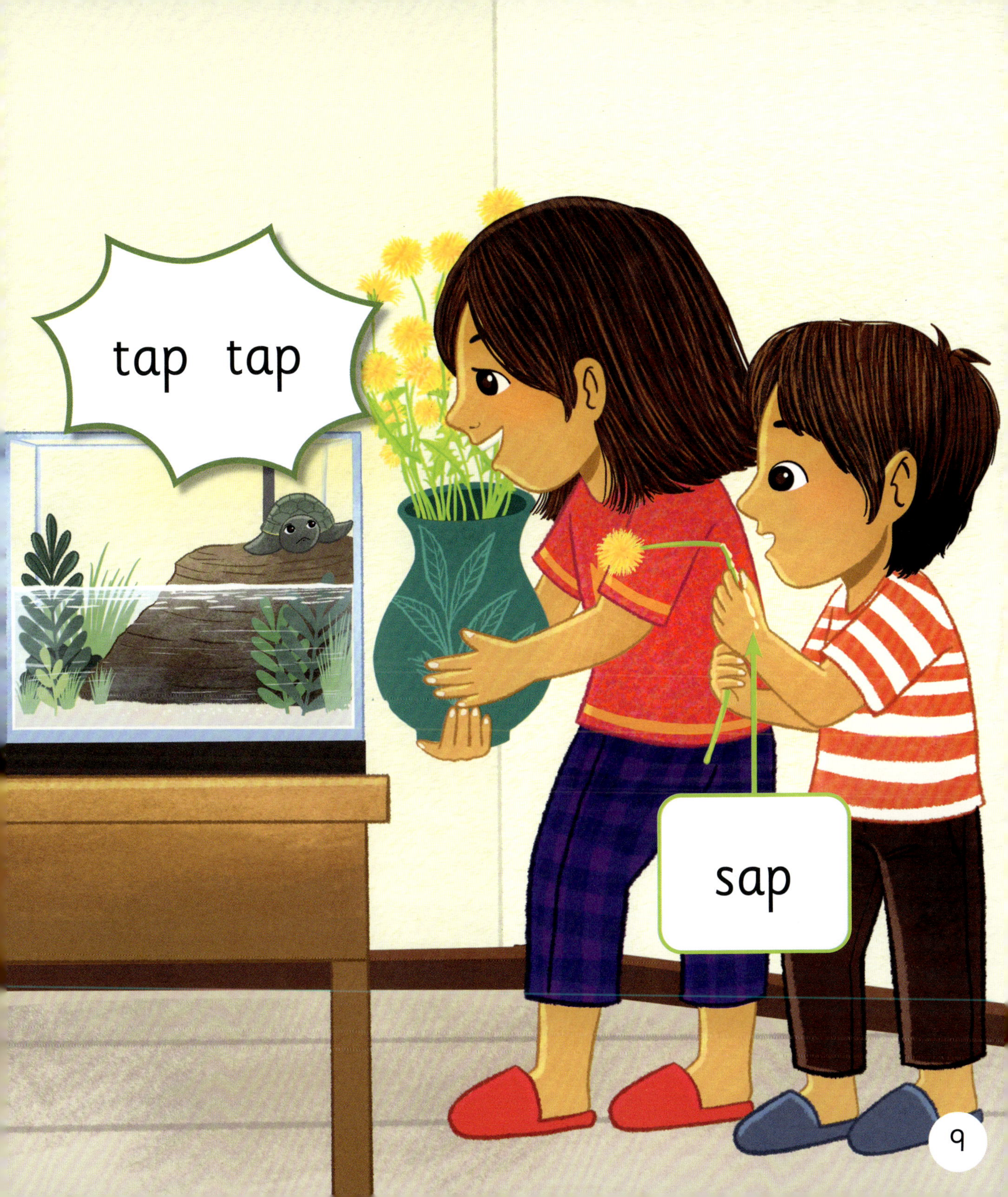
tap tap
sap

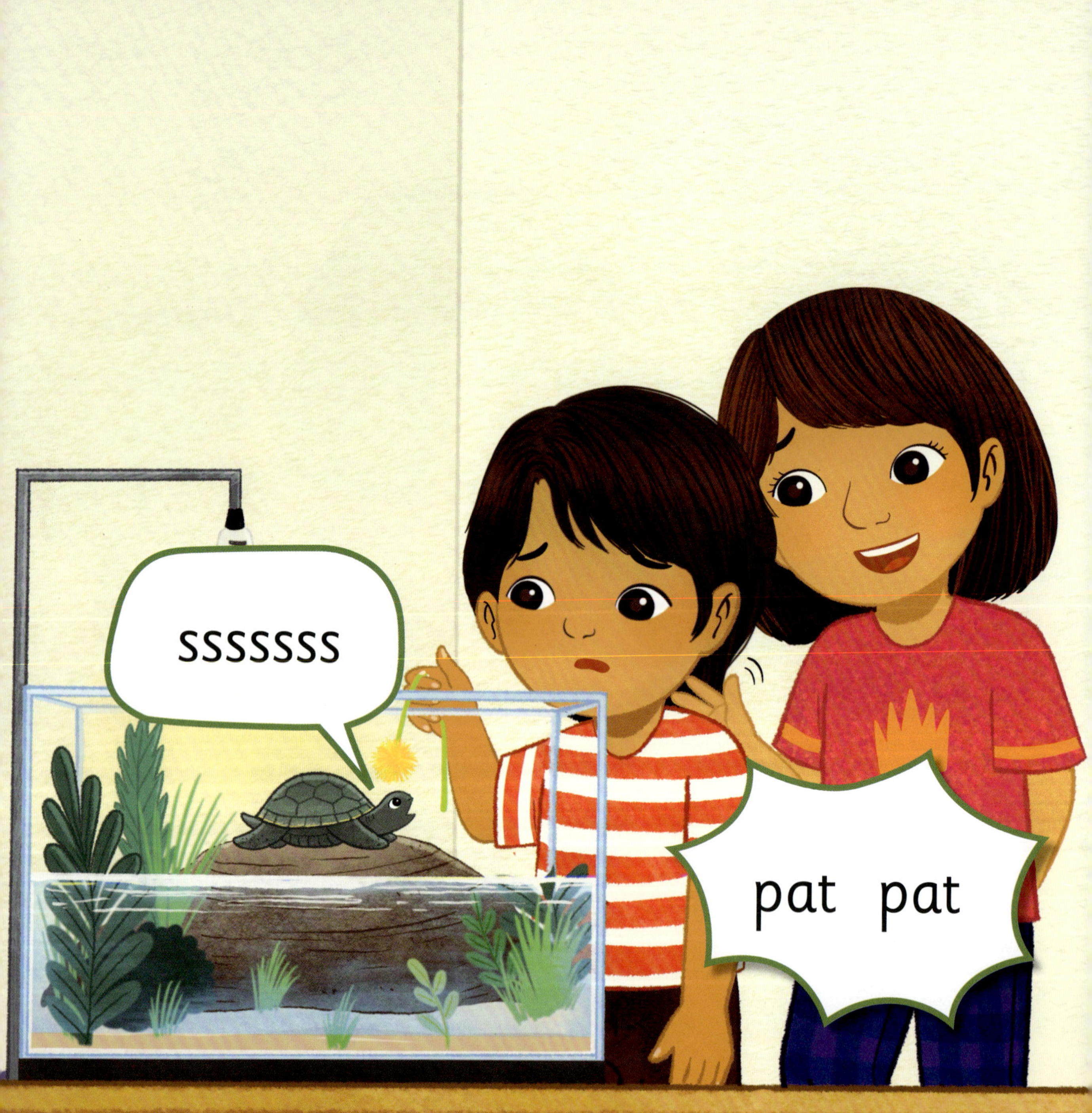
sssssss
pat pat

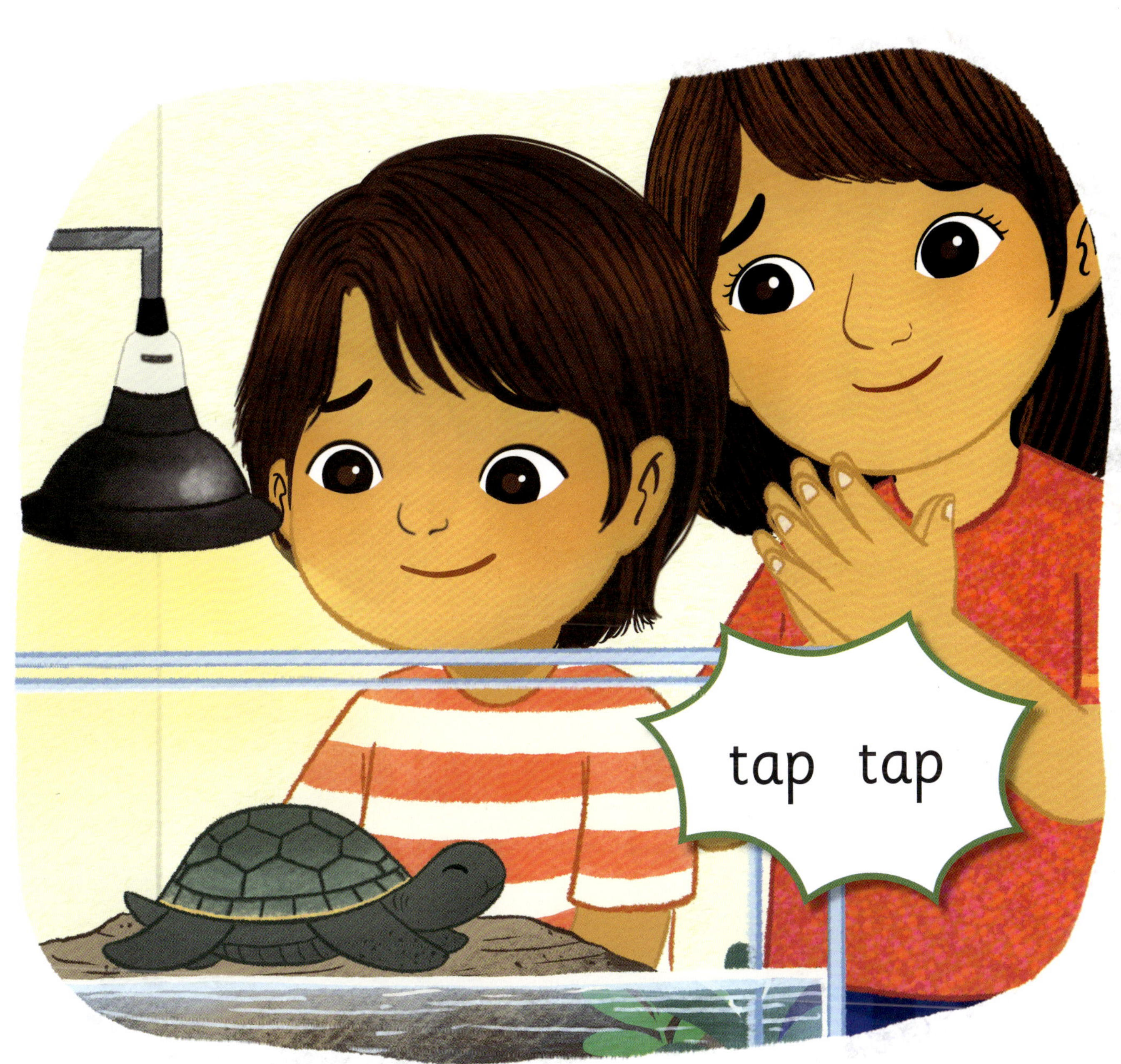
tap tap

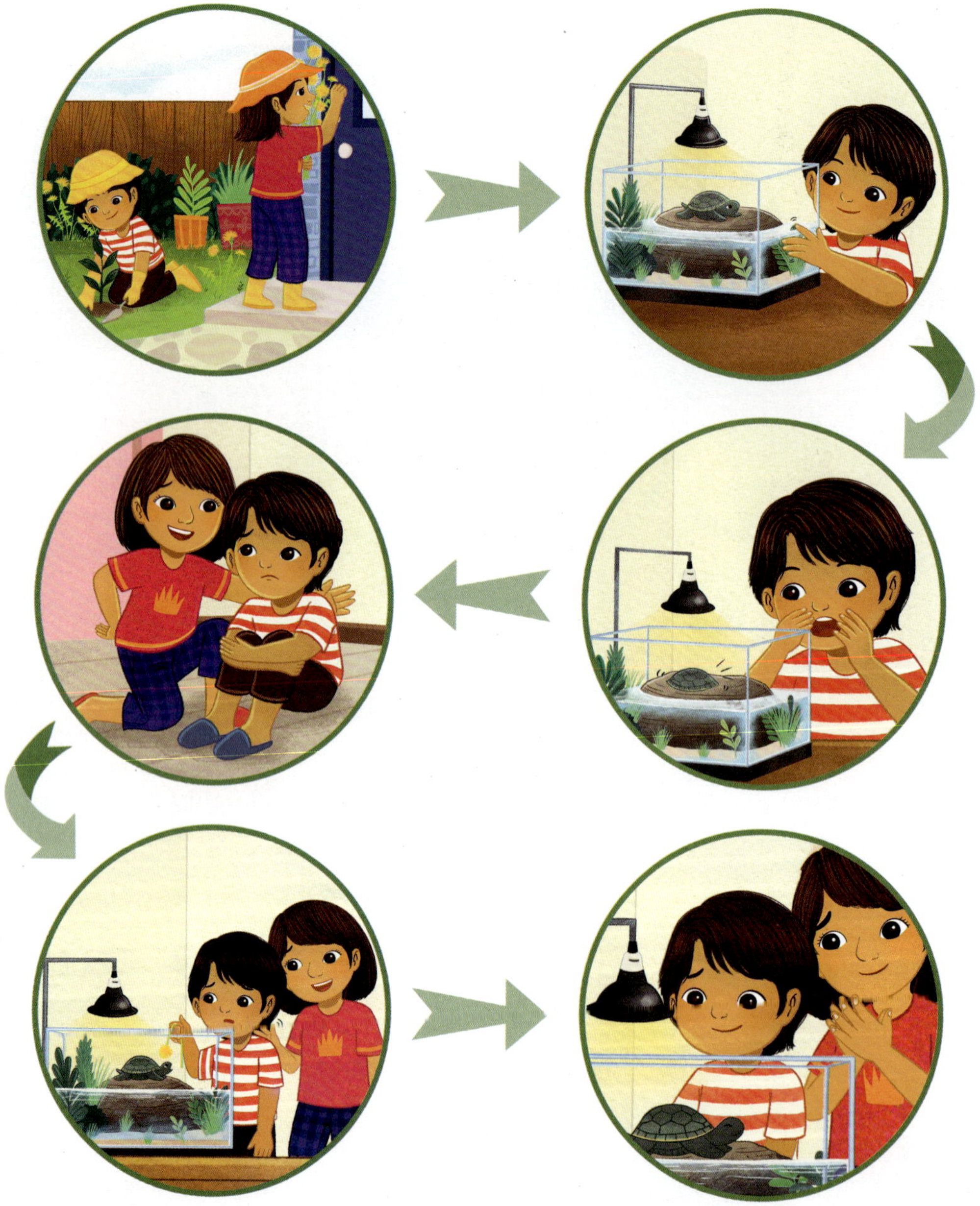

Encourage students to use the pictures to retell the story.